Composition
Skills Practice

Perfection Learning®

© 2011 Perfection Learning® Corporation

The purchase of this book entitles an individual teacher to reproduce pages for use in the classroom. This permitted use of copyrighted material does not extend beyond the building level. Reproduction for use in an entire school system or for commercial use is prohibited. Beyond the classroom use by an individual teacher, reproduction, transmittal, or retrieval of this work is prohibited without written permission from the publisher.

Printed in the United States of America.

1 2 3 4 5 6 WC 16 15 14 13 12 11

For information, contact
Perfection Learning® Corporation
1000 North Second Avenue, P.O. Box 500
Logan, Iowa 51546-0500
Phone: 1-800-831-4190 • Fax: 1-800-543-2745
perfectionlearning.com

78004
ISBN-13: 978-0-7891-8011-7
ISBN-10: 0-7891-8011-1

Table of Contents

Table of Contents *continued*

CHAPTER 1 Strategies for Finding a Subject

Exercise On a separate sheet of paper, brainstorm a list of details about each of the subjects below. Use the questions to help you.

1. Subject: my first job
   A Where did you work?
   B What skills did you use?
   C What did you learn about being a good employee?

2. Subject: my best friend
   A What qualities do you admire about your best friend?
   B How did you become friends?
   C What do you like to do together?

3. Subject: my neighborhood
   A What does it look like?
   B Who lives near you?
   C Why is it special?

4. Subject: my favorite sport
   A With whom do you play the sport?
   B What equipment do you need?
   C Where do you play?

5. Subject: my favorite food
   A What does it consist of?
   B Who serves it?
   C How does it look, taste, smell?

6. Subject: a memorable building
   A What does it look like?
   B What events have happened there?
   C What significance does it have for you?

CHAPTER 1 Choosing and Limiting a Subject

Exercise Using what you have written about the subjects in the previous exercise, choose and limit your subject.

1. Decide which of the subjects in the preceding exercise interests you the most and will also interest your readers. Write that subject below.

   _____

   _____

2. Now think of ways to limit that subject. Write the limited aspects of your subject below.

   _____

   _____

   _____

   _____

   _____

   _____

   _____

   _____

   _____

   _____

   _____

   _____

   _____

3. Choose one of these limited subjects to write about. Be sure that it is a subject that really interests you and one that you can cover adequately in the composition you are planning. On the line below, write the limited subject you have chosen.

   _____

Copyright © Perfection Learning® All rights reserved.

CHAPTER 1 Occasion, Audience, and Purpose

Exercise Answer the following questions about the limited subject you chose in the previous exercise.

1. What is the motivation, or occasion, for writing about this subject?

_____

_____

2. What is your purpose in writing? Check one of the following:

_____ to describe a place, person, object, or event

_____ to create a work of imagination

_____ to persuade your readers to share an opinion

_____ to express your thoughts and feelings

3. Who will be your audience be? Answer the following questions about the people you expect to read your work.
   A Will the audience be adults, teenagers, or children?
   B Why will my composition be of interest to them?
   C What do they already know about my subject?

_____

_____

_____

_____

   D Do they already hold some opinions about it? What opinions are they likely to hold?

_____

_____

   E Will I need to define any words or terms for them? What words or terms will need defining?

_____

_____

_____

_____

_____

Copyright © Perfection Learning® All rights reserved.

CHAPTER 1   Strategies for Developing a Subject

Exercise A Now you will develop the details that can make your writing lively and interesting. Use clustering. Write your limited subject in the rectangular hub below. Then write the first idea or detail you think of in the oval space at the end of the spoke. Continue to add spokes as you need them, writing all the ideas and details that occur to you. Remember that sometimes supporting details become new hubs with spokes of their own. Use a separate sheet of paper if necessary.

continued

   Copyright © Perfection Learning® All rights reserved.

Chapter 1: Strategies for Developing a Subject *continued*

> **Exercise B** Use questions to develop details for your essay. Here are some questions to get you started. Answer them, and add other questions that occur to you. Use another sheet of paper if you need more room.

Who will be interested in your subject?

_____

Who is directly affected by it?

_____

Why is it important?

_____

_____

How can your readers make a difference?

_____

_____

What specific actions can they take?

_____

_____

What will these actions cost in money or time?

_____

_____

What will happen if people don't take these actions?

_____

_____

What are some arguments against your view?

_____

_____

What are your answers to those arguments?

_____

_____

Copyright © Perfection Learning® All rights reserved.

CHAPTER 1   Strategies for Organizing Details

Exercise A Organize the ideas in your cluster into groups of related ideas. Name each category to show what the ideas have in common. Write those names and the ideas that go with each of them below. Use another sheet of paper if you need more room.

Category #1:

_____

_____

_____

_____

Category #2:

_____

_____

_____

_____

_____

Category #3:

_____

_____

_____

_____

_____

Exercise B Decide on the best order in which to present each group of ideas. Check the type of order that works best for your material. Then number the groups you have created above in the order in which they should be presented.

_____ chronological order

_____ spatial order

_____ order of importance

_____ order of size

_____ order of degree

Copyright © Perfection Learning® All rights reserved.

CHAPTER 1 Drafting/Revising

Exercise A Write an introduction for your composition. This introduction should arouse interest in your subject and make your readers want to know more. Write it on the lines below. Then write the rest of your composition on a separate sheet of paper. Refer to the groups of details that you prepared.

_____

_____

_____

_____

_____

_____

_____

Exercise B Reread your first draft, trying to see it and evaluate it as your readers might. Whenever you see a way to make your draft clearer and easier to follow, jot down your idea for improvement in the spaces below. Then revise your draft to include those improvements.

_____

_____

_____

_____

_____

_____

Copyright © Perfection Learning® All rights reserved.

CHAPTER 1 · Revising

Exercise A Read the following revised draft of a paragraph and then answer the following questions. Each sentence has been numbered for your convenience.

---

(1) Eating spaghetti is an art. (2) ~~Lots of my friends eat at Tony's Italian Restaurant.~~ (3) The first time I tried, the strands slid off my fork before they reached my mouth. (4) Then I learned two methods of eating spaghetti. (5) The first was to fasten the strands to my fork by twirling them around the fork. (6) The second, an easier way for me, was to simply cut the strands into small pieces. (7) I usually was too embarrassed to enjoy my dinner. (8) ~~And that's how you eat spaghetti.~~ *I can now use either strategy to eat spaghetti expertly.*

---

1. Which sentence was moved because it was out of place?

   _____

2. Which sentence was deleted because it wandered off the subject?

   _____

3. Which sentence was rewritten to make a stronger statement?

   _____

Exercise B On a separate sheet of paper, revise the following paragraph.

---

(1) Rewrite the first sentence to make the subject clearer.

(2) Remove the sentence that strays from the subject.

(3) Arrange the sentences in a logical order.

Everyone agrees that renting is a good way to start. If you rent, you won't have paid for a pair of skates you might not want after a few falls on the ice. Be sure the blades are sharp. Make sure the rental skates fit well. Otherwise, you might get discouraged and quit before giving skating a real chance. If you keep sliding sideways, your blades are probably dull. Professional skaters always have sharp blades. When you know you really like skating, then you can buy yourself a pair of good skates. Skating is easier to master if your skates have sharp blades.

    Copyright © Perfection Learning® All rights reserved.

CHAPTER 2 Choosing Vivid Words

Exercise A On the blank line, write a specific word or words to replace the underlined part in each sentence.

Example When the alarm rang, Tony <u>got out of</u> bed. _____*leaped from his*_____

1. He knew this would be a <u>really fine</u> day. _____

2. He <u>went over</u> to the window and looked outdoors. _____

3. The sun <u>shone brightly</u> in the cloudless sky. _____

4. Satisfied, he got into his tennis clothes and put on socks with <u>colored</u> stripes. _____

5. Then he rushed into the kitchen and poured himself some <u>fruit</u> juice. _____

6. Tony packed a lunch of tuna sandwiches and <u>fruit</u>. _____

7. Next, he grabbed his <u>best</u> racquet and tucked it under his arm. _____

8. He was ready for the <u>big game</u>. _____

9. For years he had <u>worked</u> toward this match. _____

10. He felt <u>sure</u> that today the championship would finally be his. _____

Exercise B On the blank line, write a fresh simile or metaphor or use specific language to replace each underlined cliché.

Example When it comes to mountain climbing, I'm not exactly <u>an old hand</u>. _____*an expert*_____

1. A group of us set off for the mountains <u>at the crack of dawn</u>. _____

2. I arrived at the trail <u>as fresh as a daisy</u>. _____

3. I'd been up so late that I'd needed <u>to recharge my batteries</u>. _____

4. Before long on the trail, though, my legs <u>turned to jelly</u>. _____

5. Even worse, I was feeling <u>as hungry as a bear</u>. _____

Copyright © Perfection Learning® All rights reserved.

CHAPTER 2   Using Figurative Language

Exercise Follow the instructions to write sentences using figurative language.

1. Use a simile to describe a gold ring.

   _____

2. Use a metaphor to compare an emotion to a submarine.

   _____

3. Use a simile to describe a cold wind.

   _____

4. Use a simile to describe a professional basketball player.

   _____

5. Use a metaphor to compare an aroma to an intruder.

   _____

6. Use a simile to describe a sneeze.

   _____

7. Use a simile to describe a boring movie.

   _____

8. Use a simile to describe doing homework.

   _____

9. Use a metaphor to compare a football team to something in nature.

   _____

10. Use a simile to describe a cooked egg.

   _____

 Copyright © Perfection Learning® All rights reserved.

CHAPTER 2 Combining Sentences by Coordinating

Exercise Use the word given in parentheses to combine subjects, predicates, or entire sentences.

1. Some deserts are flat and sandy. Others are rocky and uneven. (but)

_____

_____

2. South America has deserts. Africa has deserts. (and)

_____

3. At an oasis, desert travelers can rest. Travelers can find water there too. (or)

_____

_____

4. Plants rarely live in sandy deserts. Winds constantly shift the sands. (for)

_____

_____

5. You should not travel in the desert without a guide. You should not leave the roads. (nor)

_____

6. The sun is extremely hot in many deserts. Small animals burrow under the sand. (so)

_____

_____

7. Small desert animals drink no water. They must get moisture from somewhere. (yet)

_____

_____

8. Extreme heat can characterize a desert. Extreme cold can too. (or)

_____

9. Camels can travel long distances. Camels can go without water. (and)

_____

10. Six continents contain desert areas. Europe does not. (but)

_____

Copyright © Perfection Learning® All rights reserved.

CHAPTER 2 Combining Sentences by Subordinating

Exercise Combine each pair of sentences by using a subordinate clause introduced by the joining word given in parentheses.

1. The steamer sails down the Niagara River. The river is famous for its Horseshoe Falls. (which)

   _____

   _____

2. The passengers wear raincoats. They exclaim in wonder at the sight and sound of the falls. (who)

   _____

   _____

3. The torrents of water splash the passengers. Children shriek with laughter. (whenever)

   _____

4. The famous boat ride has been operating since 1846. It has become a local tradition. (because)

   _____

5. Chabert Joncaire, Jr., was an early resident of the area. He used the falls to run his sawmill. (who)

   _____

   _____

6. The Niagara River follows a 35-mile path. It leads from Lake Erie to Lake Ontario. (that)

   _____

7. The American Falls, on the American side, is slightly higher. Horseshoe Falls, on the Canadian side, is far larger. (although)

   _____

   _____

8. Large electric power generators were built in the 1890s. Companies that needed a lot of electricity built plants near Niagara Falls. (after)

   _____

   _____

9. A steamer takes visitors down the river. It is named *The Maid of the Mist*. (whose)

   _____

   _____

   Copyright © Perfection Learning® All rights reserved.

CHAPTER 2 Varying Sentence Beginnings

Exercise Rewrite each sentence, using the type of opener indicated in parentheses.

1. George Catlin, the American artist, wanted the wonderful lands he saw in the West to be turned into national parks. (appositive phrase)

   _____

   _____

2. The creation of national parks was at that time a wholly new and daring idea. (prepositional phrase)

   _____

3. His wish began to come true when Yellowstone Park was created in 1872. (adverb clause)

   _____

4. Many more lands became national parklands in the years that followed. (prepositional phrase)

   _____

5. The national park system is huge today, covering more than 50 million acres. (participial phrase)

   _____

6. Some 300 million people visit the parks each year, taking advantage of this great national resource. (participial phrase)

   _____

   _____

7. George Catlin probably never imagined such heavy usage of the parklands in his visions of the future. (prepositional phrase)

   _____

   _____

8. This is both a happy and an unhappy outcome as park management people see it. (clause)

   _____

9. Overuse of the parks threatens to become a problem, since the number of users steadily increases. (adverb clause)

   _____

10. It may be necessary to create still more parklands to keep up with the ever-growing number of users. (infinitive phrase)

    _____

    _____

Copyright © Perfection Learning® All rights reserved.

CHAPTER 2   Varying Sentence Structure

Exercise Combine the sentences in each group into a single sentence. Use the sentence structure indicated in parentheses.

1. The speeches of one man were considered models for public speakers. This was true for more than 2,000 years. (simple)

   _____

   _____

2. This man was Demosthenes. He was a Greek. He lived in the 4th century B.C. (complex)

   _____

   _____

3. Demosthenes had a problem as a youth. He stuttered badly. (simple)

   _____

4. Legend says that he practiced speaking with a mouthful of pebbles. This cured the stutter. (compound-complex)

   _____

   _____

5. After that, he took up oratory. He became the greatest orator that Greece had ever known. (compound-complex)

   _____

   _____

6. Several of his speeches denounce one man. That man is King Philip of Macedonia. (simple)

   _____

   _____

7. Today, we still use the word *philipic*. We use it to mean any bitter verbal attack. (simple)

   _____

   _____

8. One thing is clear. Demosthenes left a lasting mark on the world. (complex)

   _____

   Copyright © Perfection Learning® All rights reserved.

CHAPTER 2 **Revising and Combining Sentences**

Exercise Revise the sentences below by correcting the problems indicated in parentheses.

1. Every autumn thousands of eels leave European rivers. They travel across the Atlantic Ocean. They go to Bermuda. They lay their eggs there. (No variation in sentence structure)

   _____

   _____

   _____

2. After the eggs hatch, the Gulf Stream transports them back to the coast of Europe, and when they get there they become elvers, which is what young eels are called, and they go back into the rivers and other fresh waters. (Rambling)

   _____

   _____

   _____

3. They live there for ten years. They grow into adult eels. They make the same journey their parents made. (No variation in sentence structure)

   _____

   _____

4. Other eels spawn in Bermuda too, and when their turn to migrate comes, these American eels make the journey to the waters where they will produce their young. (Rambling)

   _____

   _____

   _____

5. Some mysterious instinct leads the newborn American eels back to the home waters of their parents exactly as it draws the European eels back to their homes, and the cycle is complete. (Rambling)

   _____

   _____

   _____

   _____

• • • CHAPTER 2 Revising Rambling Sentences

Exercise Rewrite each rambling sentence below. Separate the ideas into a mixture of short and long sentences.

1. Niagara Falls has attracted and awed visitors for over a century and a half, and to allow people to appreciate the power and beauty of the falls, towers, bridges, caves, and boats have been provided, and as a result tourists can view the spectacle from almost any angle.

_____

_____

_____

_____

_____

2. Visitors who want to look down on the splendid sight can do so because four towers have been built that overlook the falls, but if people prefer to look up at the thundering water, they can also do that if they take the steamer that sails around the base of the falls, or they can descend 125 feet in an elevator and look out from behind the falls.

_____

_____

_____

_____

_____

_____

_____

3. Near the northern end of the Niagara River are the Whirlpool Rapids, where the onrushing rapids crash, bounce, and whirl around a basin that they have carved in the rock and that can be seen from a cableway that carries visitors directly over the whirlpool.

_____

_____

_____

_____

_____

Copyright © Perfection Learning® All rights reserved.

CHAPTER 2 Writing Concise Sentences

> **Exercise A** On the blank line, write *R* if the sentence contains a redundancy. Write *EE* if the sentence contains an empty expression. Then underline the word or words that should be eliminated.

Example The Amazon River is longer <u>in length</u> than the Mississippi.   R

1. What I mean is that I didn't do my homework last night.   _____

2. Jill and Sam together made supper for all of us.   _____

3. Is a navel orange sweeter in taste than other oranges?   _____

4. Today's game has been canceled because of the fact that rain is predicted.   _____

5. It is true that many people are color-blind.   _____

6. The thing is that my tennis shoes are worn out.   _____

7. The fact is that I think Arabian horses run faster than Percherons.   _____

8. Loren is positively certain that he lost his notebook on the street.   _____

9. The round, full moon rose over the mountains.   _____

10. The tall six-footer tried out for the basketball team.   _____

> **Exercise B** On the blank line, revise each sentence by shortening the wordy phrase or clause.

Example Apples that have been dried can be used in cooking.

    Dried apples can be used in cooking.

1. Tourists in Mexico can visit many ancient pyramids <u>that are made of stone</u>.

   _____

2. Brazil, <u>which is the fifth largest country in the world</u>, covers half of South America.

   _____

3. Animals <u>that live in the desert</u> usually sleep in the shade during the day.

   _____

4. Do you like the smell of bread <u>that has been freshly baked</u>?

   _____

5. The trainer handled the horses <u>in a firm manner</u>.

   _____

Copyright © Perfection Learning® All rights reserved.

CHAPTER 2 Revising Sentences to Make Them Concise

Exercise Rewrite each sentence to make it more concise.

1. It is known by most people that too much fat in the diet is unhealthful.

   _____

2. Nevertheless, the fact is that fats are a basic food, along with proteins and carbohydrates.

   _____

   _____

3. Without any fat at all, a person would eventually die.

   _____

4. Fats that are edible are found in animal and plant tissues, especially in seeds.

   _____

5. Fat supplies more than twice as much fuel as the same identical amount of protein or carbohydrate.

   _____

   _____

6. The thing is that fats give off a great deal of heat as they are used by the body.

   _____

7. People who live in warm climates, therefore, need less fat than those in cold climates.

   _____

8. When more fat is eaten than is burned up by the body, the excess that is not used is stored in the tissues.

   _____

   _____

9. Digestive juices take a long time to break down fats slowly.

   _____

10. Fried foods, due to the fact that they are covered with fat, are digested more slowly than boiled or broiled foods are.

    _____

    _____

  Copyright © Perfection Learning® All rights reserved.

CHAPTER 2 **Revising to Eliminate Redundancy and Empty Expressions**

Exercise Rewrite the sentences below, removing redundant or empty expressions.

1. Maria removed all superfluous and unnecessary details from her drawing.

   _____

2. The changes left her with what was a clean and striking sketch of the view from her bedroom window.

   _____

   _____

3. Due to the fact that the view was of a city street, it contained many sharp angles.

   _____

4. Perhaps it was the past history of her family that gave Maria her eye for line and color.

   _____

   _____

5. It seemed as if transferring the sketch to canvas was extremely difficult for Maria.

   _____

   _____

6. There was a softness in the paintbrush and the colors that rounded the angles and mellowed the entire scene.

   _____

   _____

7. She asked the art teacher to let her try and attempt to work with clay.

   _____

   _____

8. The thing that she liked best was the feel of the clay as it softened.

   _____

9. What she wanted was to let the clay itself determine what she would make.

   _____

   _____

10. Each and every single moment in the art room was interesting and exciting for her.

   _____

   _____

Copyright © Perfection Learning® All rights reserved.

CHAPTER 2 Replacing Clichés

Exercise Rewrite each sentence, replacing the underlined cliché with a fresh comparison.

1. The sunburn left Bert <u>as red as a beet</u>.

_____

2. His mouth felt <u>as dry as dust</u>.

_____

3. Today it was <u>raining cats and dogs</u>.

_____

4. In a month, a <u>blanket of snow</u> would cover the ground.

_____

_____

5. Bert was <u>down in the dumps</u>.

_____

6. Was he <u>making a mountain out of a molehill</u>?

_____

7. After all, life wasn't just <u>a bowl of cherries</u>.

_____

8. He would be <u>as quiet as a mouse</u> and not complain.

_____

_____

9. He knew he shouldn't be <u>green with envy</u>.

_____

10. Everyone in the family was being <u>as nice as pie</u> to him.

_____

_____

   Copyright © Perfection Learning® All rights reserved.

CHAPTER 2 Using Words with Positive and Negative Connotations

Exercise In each sentence a choice of words is given in brackets. On the blank line, write the word with the specified connotation.

1. There was much [excitement, agitation] as our family prepared for its first trip to Greece. (positive)

   _____

2. In Athens we were joined by Uncle Ted, who was [fatter, more portly] than I expected. (negative)

   _____

3. He had a [loud, hearty] voice that caused everyone to notice him. (positive)

   _____

4. "I can't wait to show you the [wreckage, remains] of this fabulous civilization," he told us. (positive)

   _____

5. Uncle Ted teaches history and is filled with [enthusiasm, fanaticism] about the past. (positive)

   _____

6. He took us to historic sites and gave us [extensive, long-winded] explanations of everything. (negative)

   _____

7. When he told us about the Trojan War, he said that most tales were [fictitious, legendary]. (positive)

   _____

8. Later, we enjoyed Greek music with the [raucous, lively] Athenian crowds. (positive)

   _____

9. I tried to [please, flatter] the Greeks I met by using a few Greek words I had learned. (positive)

   _____

10. At lunch we were [forced, obliged] to try some foods we had never heard of before. (negative)

    _____

11. Some of these foods tasted very [weird, exotic] to us. (positive)

    _____

12. Flying home, we talked about the adventures we had [experienced, undergone] in Greece. (positive)

    _____

Copyright © Perfection Learning® All rights reserved.

CHAPTER 3   Paragraph Structure

> **Exercise A** One topic sentence in each pair is limited enough to be covered in one paragraph. On the blank line, write the letter identifying that sentence.

Example   *b*   a. The local restaurant is our meeting place.
                      b. Every afternoon Tony's Pizza Palace is filled with kids from our school.

_____ 1.   a. Some streams are not good for fishing.
               b. Don't try fly casting on the tree-bordered Cataloochee River.

_____ 2.   a. My 150-pound Saint Bernard is an ideal companion.
               b. Some dogs are better than others.

_____ 3.   a. I like to cook.
               b. Crusty rye bread is my baking specialty.

_____ 4.   a. A successful apple grower keeps a detailed pruning and spraying schedule.
               b. Fruit trees need a lot of care.

_____ 5.   a. More than half our living tissue is water.
               b. Water is the most familiar liquid on earth.

> **Exercise B** On the blank lines, write two different concluding sentences for the paragraph below.

> Most people pull up weeds, but one man devoted an entire book to defending weeds. He pointed out that weeds provide minerals to the soil. They also offer useful indications of soil conditions. Of course, many weeds can be eaten. Dandelion greens make delicious vegetable dishes. Many weeds are picked for their beauty and are used in bouquets and flower arrangements. Dried flower arrangements are often made entirely of weeds. Weeds have also been used to make medicines. Some are made into ointments to cure skin problems; other have been made into medicines to be taken internally.

1. _____

_____

2. _____

_____

      Copyright © Perfection Learning® All rights reserved.

• • • ⬤ CHAPTER 3 ⬤ Unity and Coherence

Exercise A Decide which two sentences in each paragraph stray from the subject. Then draw a line through each sentence.

---

1.   More and more people are taking their vacations in the underwater world. Mammals also inhabit this world. They live on fish. There are two kinds of sport diving: snorkeling and scuba diving. Snorkelers wear face masks, short snorkel breathing tubes, and swim fins. Scuba divers carry portable tanks of compressed air strapped to their backs and wear a variety of additional equipment. Both well-equipped snorkelers and scuba divers can take underwater photos, explore reefs, swim among fish, and hunt for buried treasure. Divers have fun and relax completely in their quiet, buoyant worlds.

2.   Bumblebees are priceless friends of human beings. They are the only creatures that can fertilize red clover, a very valuable crop. They alone are equipped to reach inside the red clover flowers. You have probably seen banks of red clover. It often grows wild along highways. Bumblebees have to keep working because they store very little honey. A bumblebee's life is limited to one summer. Only the queen secretes the substance that enables her to live through the winter. In the spring, in her underground burrow, she lays the eggs that develop into her busy family, so useful to humans.

Exercise B On each blank line, write a transition that makes the order of ideas clear. Use the lists below.

TRANSITIONS: Second, Before, First, Finally, Third

1. _____ beginning an all-day hike, make sure you are dressed properly.

2. _____ , make sure the clothing you have will be warm enough.

3. _____ , wear layers of clothing that can be added or removed as the temperature changes.

4. _____ , comfortable hiking shoes are the best defense against aching feet and sprained ankles.

5. _____ , lightweight rain gear will help keep you comfortable.

TRANSITIONS: At the top, At the bottom, In the center, In front of

6. _____ our porch we hung a hummingbird feeder under the eaves.

7. _____ of the feeder is a clear plastic string used for hanging it.

8. _____ of the feeder is a clear tube that holds a quart of sugar water.

9. _____ are four plastic flowers that release the liquid.

Copyright © Perfection Learning® All rights reserved.

CHAPTER 3 Choosing and Limiting a Subject

Suppose that your local hospital is preparing a pamphlet on nutrition for the general public. You have been asked to write a paragraph on popcorn, which will be included in a chapter on snack foods.

Notes on Popcorn for Nutrition Pamphlet

1. Consumption of popcorn has nearly doubled in last decade
2. Used by South Americans 2,000 years ago for food and decoration
3. Charles Cretors, Chicago, invented first popping machine in late 1800s
4. Popcorn not only tastes good but is good for you
5. Added butter means lots of added calories
6. High in complex carbohydrates and fiber, which doctors recommend
7. Cup popped in oil, unbuttered = about 40 calories
8. Contains iron, B vitamins, some protein
9. Introduced by American Indians to Pilgrim settlers
10. Cup popped in hot air and unbuttered = only 23 calories
11. Early popping machines put on wagons, and popcorn sold on streets
12. Beware—flavors, candy coatings, and butter raise calorie count significantly
13. American Dental Association: popcorn cleans teeth
14. Now available in dozens of fancy flavors
15. By 1980s, 611 million pounds of popcorn consumed annually in U.S.
16. Can easily be popped at home—in fireplace, on stove, in electric popper, in microwave
17. Kernels heated; moisture inside changes to steam
18. Kernel explodes from pressure of steam
19. Home popping machines available that pop with hot air only, not oil
20. Cup popped in hot air and unbuttered = 23 calories, same as medium raw carrot, one bite of cheese, or third of a very small apple, but more filling
21. Oil used to pop because helps distribute heat evenly around kernels
22. Cup of kernels expands to 30 to 40 cups popped

Exercise Complete the list below, ending with three clearly focused subjects that are suggested by the research notes on popcorn.

1. **Limited Subject** _____

2. **More Limited Subject** _____

3. **Suitably Limited Subject** _____

   Copyright © Perfection Learning® All rights reserved.

CHAPTER 3 Developing Supporting Details; Arranging Details in Logical Order

> **Exercise A** Choose two focused subjects from the exercise on page 24. Select details from the notes that would help you to explain each subject. List the details in the order in which they appear in the notes.

1. **FOCUSED SUBJECT I** _____

   Details I _____

   _____

   _____

   _____

2. **FOCUSED SUBJECT II** _____

   Details II _____

   _____

   _____

   _____

> **Exercise B** Arrange the details you listed in the previous exercise in a logical order. Identify your method of organization: *chronological order, spatial order, order of importance, order of interest*, or *order of degree*.

1. **LIST I** _____

   _____

   _____

   _____

   Method of Organization I _____

2. **LIST II** _____

   _____

   _____

   _____

   Method of Organization II _____

CHAPTER 3 Classifying Supporting Details

Exercise On the blank lines, write whether the details are *descriptive details, reasons, comparison/contrast,* or *steps in a process.*

_____ 1. Growing a fruit tree in a pot is surprisingly easy. After eating an orange or a grapefruit, save the seeds. Soak the seeds in water overnight. Then plant them one-quarter inch deep in a pot of soil. The soil should include a layer of gravel on the bottom, covered by a layer of sand. Then peat moss and a top layer of rich soil should be added. Place the pot in a sunny window, and water it lightly if the soil feels dry. Soon you will have tiny trees. Place each tree in a separate pot, and watch them grow.

_____ 2. Kayaks and speedboats are both watercraft, but they are usually used for different purposes. Kayaks move quietly and slowly through water, propelled by muscle power; however, speedboats are propelled by gasoline engines and usually move very fast. Gliding along quietly in a kayak gives a paddler exercise and a chance to view the scenery and wildlife closely. Speedboats, on the other hand, provide an easy, fast method of getting from one spot to another. In different ways, each can prove useful on a lake, pond, or river.

_____ 3. Researchers have found that people with pets live longer, happier lives. Of course, owners of pets have known all along that they are much happier when they have a pet to keep them company. Having an animal to care for makes a person feel needed. Pets, after all, are totally dependent on their owners for food, care, and affection. Also, when people are lonely or housebound, a pet can provide companionship. Perhaps most important, giving care to a pet and receiving love in return helps people feel more content.

_____ 4. The hope chest at the foot of my grandmother's bed is full of wonderful treasures. In one corner, carefully tied with blue ribbons, are letters my mother wrote as a child. Two albums contain pictures and old newspaper clippings, carefully arranged in chronological order. One box is filled with menus, dried flowers, programs, and other mementos of happy occasions. At the very bottom of the chest is Grandmother's wedding dress, folded neatly in blue tissue in a box. Every item reminds her of some special occasion, friend, or much-loved relative.

  Copyright © Perfection Learning® All rights reserved.

••• **CHAPTER 3** **Arranging Details in Logical Order**

> **Exercise** Identify the method of organization used in each paragraph. Write *chronological*, *spatial*, or *importance* on the blank line.

_____ 1. On the cliffs of North Devon in England, sheep once grazed. Colonies of ants thrived in the meadows kept short by the sheep. These ants would find the eggs of the rare Large Blue butterfly, mistake them for their own eggs, and take them to their underground homes. As the butterfly caterpillars developed from these eggs, they ate the ants. Finally they came out of the burrows as Large Blue butterflies. Now the sheep are gone; ants cannot survive in the long grasses; and these butterflies are extinct.

_____ 2. Bandelier National Monument is a deep canyon in New Mexico where Indians lived in prehistoric times. As you walk from the ranger station along the creek, you see the stone foundations of many rooms and of great circular kivas, ceremonial structures. Then the trail leads up to the base of a vertical cliff on your right. In this cliff of volcanic rock are many caves. Further on, high above the trail, there are small caves where some of the Indians lived. At the end of this part of the canyon, 114 feet above the stream, is a large cave, probably used for tribal ceremonies.

_____ 3. Postal systems increased in importance as more people wrote to each other. At first the systems existed only for a few rulers and nobles. As more and more people engaged in business, regularly scheduled mail routes were set up. Private companies handled these at first; as the volume of mail increased, governments took over the job. Now the Universal Postal Union, an organization of the United Nations, regulates international mail service.

_____ 4. Portugal, a country in Europe about the size of Maine, is divided into three regions. North of the Tagus River is a mountainous area covered with forests of pine and oak. The vineyards in some of the valleys here are famous for producing delicious grapes. Gently rolling plains extend south of the Tagus, where olive trees and cork oaks flourish. Half the world's supply of cork comes from these trees. Along the southern coast lie some of the world's most beautiful beaches. This region is called the Algarve.

Copyright © Perfection Learning® All rights reserved.

CHAPTER 3 Drafting the Topic Sentence, Body, and Concluding Sentence

---

Exercise A Write a topic sentence that expresses the main idea of each list you made on page 25.

1. **TOPIC SENTENCE I**

   _____

2. **TOPIC SENTENCE II**

   _____

Exercise B Using your topic sentences and organized details, write two paragraphs about popcorn on a separate sheet of paper. Write a complete sentence for each detail. Then combine sentences that go together. Leave room for concluding sentences.

Exercise C Write a sentence to conclude each paragraph you previously wrote. Then identify the function of your sentence.

   a. restates the main idea   **c.** evaluates the details
   b. summarizes the paragraph   **d.** adds an insight

1. **CONCLUDING SENTENCE I**

   _____

2. **CONCLUDING SENTENCE II**

   _____

Exercise D Check your paragraphs for unity and coherence. In addition, carefully check for correct grammar and usage, spelling, capitalization, and punctuation.

Copyright © Perfection Learning® All rights reserved.

CHAPTER 4   Drawing on Personal Experience

Exercise From your personal experience, choose a subject for a personal essay. Here are possible sources of ideas:

childhood learning experiences   visits to favorite places
school events   holidays or vacations
interaction with relatives or friends   experiences concerning sports or hobbies
favorite things

After choosing your subject, complete the following statements.

1. This experience is important to me now because

_____

_____

_____

_____

2. I will always remember this experience because

_____

_____

_____

_____

3. This experience is worth writing about because

_____

_____

_____

_____

Copyright © Perfection Learning® All rights reserved.

CHAPTER 4 Developing Narrative Paragraphs

> **Exercise A** On the blank line, write *first person* or *third person* to tell the point of view in each sentence.

Example   One night last summer, I climbed a mountain in total darkness. One of the people I was climbing with hadn't returned to camp with the rest of us.

first person

1. The door flew open and in stepped Rod, with a bouquet and a big grin.

_____

2. She poured ice water into each container and handed one to each of us to carry in our knapsacks.

_____

3. I joined the others in front of the microscope. Each of us took a turn looking through the lens at the slide of pond water.

_____

4. When the plane stopped, we all gathered our belongings and headed for the exit.

_____

5. Nancy sat alone in the back of the theater, watching carefully each gesture the actors made.

_____

6. When I told my parents I wanted to try out for the tennis team, they bought me a new racquet.

_____

7. Every year Travel Club members raise money so that they can spend a weekend in Washington.

_____

8. When I was sixteen, I started taking driving lessons.

_____

9. Our parents limit us to one hour of TV watching on weekdays.

_____

10. Some people think the 21st century started on January 1, 2000.

_____

> **Exercise B** On a separate sheet of paper, write a narrative paragraph. Use one of the topic sentences below or one of your own. Remember to develop details by brainstorming answers to the following questions: *Who? What? When? Why? Where? How?*

(1) I'll always remember my last term's grades.

(2) When the creaking noise first began, I sat petrified.

(3) As the band began to play, I spun my baton.

(4) "Get down in front!" yelled one angry fan.

(5) As we peered out the window, the sound became deafening.

> **Exercise C** Revise your paragraph and edit the revision carefully. Then prepare a neat final copy.

   Copyright © Perfection Learning® All rights reserved.

CHAPTER 4 Organizing Details

Exercise Identify the type of order used in each paragraph by writing on the blank line *spatial*, *importance*, *chronological*, or *developmental*.

_____   1. During my first six years, we lived in the upstairs apartment of a two-family house on Mott Street. The house was near St. Mark's Hospital, where my mother worked as a maternity ward nurse. I had many friends of all ages in our neighborhood, but I was closest to Tommy, a classmate of mine. After my mother got a supervisor's job in Simpson Hospital, we moved across town to a beautiful new apartment building on Barrow Street.

_____   2. Our new corner apartment was on the fifth floor. From our living room window, we had a view across rooftops toward the Mackinaw River. The kitchen was big and sunny, with windows toward the east and south. My mother put up two glass shelves in the south window and filled them with pots of geraniums and African violets. On sunny mornings the kitchen was filled with a warm golden light.

_____   3. The new apartment was ideally situated for me. In the first place, Hanson Park was located only three blocks away. That's where my friends and I played softball on warm evenings and ice-skated on winter afternoons. Better yet, I was three blocks closer to school, which meant I could stay in bed five minutes longer on school mornings. Best of all, my mother worked just around the corner, so we saw much more of each other. That meant she had more time to bake delicious cookies and pies and had free time to go to the movies with me.

_____   4. Tommy lived farther away, but we still managed to get together at school, since we were both in the same school district. He usually took the bus over to my place on Sunday afternoons. On rainy days we both liked to build model airplanes. On sunny days we often rode our bikes through the park to the zoo.

Copyright © Perfection Learning® All rights reserved.

CHAPTER 4 Supporting Details

Exercise Revise the following paragraphs by adding details that would help readers to visualize or understand the experience. Use the questions following each paragraph to help you decide which details to add.

1. When we finally reached the restaurant, we were all starving. We rushed inside the cool interior and arranged ourselves in a comfortable booth near the counter. After reading the menu, we each ordered. The restaurant was not very busy so our waitress brought our food quickly. No meal had ever tasted more delicious to me.

   Who was with you?

   What restaurant did you go to?

   What did you each order?

   How soon did the meals arrive?

   _____

   _____

   _____

   _____

   _____

   _____

   _____

2. The waitress turned out to be a relative of mine. She looked very capable in her snappy uniform. We greeted each other and then I introduced her to everyone. She told us what dish was especially tasty and two of us ordered it.

   What relative was she?

   What was her uniform like?

   How did you greet her?

   What dish was especially tasty?

   Who ordered it?

   _____

   _____

   _____

   _____

   _____

Copyright © Perfection Learning® All rights reserved.

CHAPTER 4 Writing Narrative Paragraphs

Exercise Suppose that you work for an advertising agency that is launching a new brand of vitamins. Your assignment is to write a narrative paragraph, using the memo below and the steps that follow.

CARY, WEISS & BOWMAN ADVERTISING, INC.

Account: Amazon-Plus Vitamins

Strategy: The aim of the advertising campaign will be to associate these vitamins with super strength. The approach will be humorous. Every week a one-paragraph story will appear in selected newspapers and magazines. It will be styled and written like a regular news article even though it will be clearly labeled as an advertisement. The paragraph will tell what happened when, after taking an Amazon-Plus vitamin daily for a few days, a particular person suddenly developed super strength. The tone and events should be kept light and humorous, though not silly. We want readers to look forward to reading about the exploits of a new Amazon-Plus superhero each week.

---

1. Decide on a point of view. Check the point of view you choose.

   _____ a. first person   _____ b. third person

2. On a separate sheet of paper, write your supporting sentences in chronological order. Use transitions to show how the events are related in time.

3. Check the purpose you choose. Then write your topic sentence.

   _____ a. make a general statement   _____ b. capture attention   _____ c. set the scene

   TOPIC SENTENCE:

   _____

   _____

   _____

4. Check the purpose you choose. Then write your concluding sentence.

   _____ a. summarize   _____ b. make a point

   CONCLUDING SENTENCE:

   _____

   _____

   _____

5. Add the topic sentence and the concluding sentence to the supporting sentences.

6. Revise and edit your paragraph.

Copyright © Perfection Learning® All rights reserved.

• • • CHAPTER 5   Specific Details and Sensory Words

Exercise A Rewrite the following sentences, replacing the underlined sections with more specific words or details.

Example   Ernesto and I went to the zoo to see the <u>interesting animal show</u>.

Ernesto and I went to the zoo to see the wild elephant spectacle.

1. The interior of their new car has <u>some unique features</u>.

   _____

2. After Karen finished cleaning, the kitchen <u>looked clean</u>.

   _____

3. That lasagna <u>smells good</u>.

   _____

4. <u>The attractive lady</u> danced the fox trot.

   _____

5. Madeline wore <u>strange clothes</u> to the banquet.

   _____

6. Their production of *The King and I* was not <u>very good</u>.

   _____

7. My friend John got <u>an odd haircut</u>.

   _____

8. <u>That neat dog</u> can jump through hoops.

   _____

9. She lent me <u>that good book by that great author</u>.

   _____

10. What do you think of <u>the color of my clothes</u>?

    _____

continued

   Copyright © Perfection Learning® All rights reserved.

Chapter 5: Specific Details and Sensory Words *continued*

Exercise B Read the following four words or groups of words. Then write two specific examples of sights, sounds, smells, tastes, and feelings that can describe each item. Be as detailed and evocative as possible in your list of sensory details.

Example a swimming pool

Sights _kids splashing water_

Sounds _squeals of delight, rushing water_

Smells _chlorine_

Tastes _candy from concession stand_

Feelings _exhaustion_

1. a carnival

Sights _____

Sounds _____

Smells _____

Tastes _____

Feelings _____

2. a new puppy

Sights _____

Sounds _____

Smells _____

Tastes _____

Feelings _____

3. a trip to the grocery store

Sights _____

Sounds _____

Smells _____

Tastes _____

Feelings _____

Copyright © Perfection Learning® All rights reserved.

CHAPTER 5 Figurative Language

> **Exercise A** For the following sentences, identify what type of figurative language is being used. On the blank line, write *S* for simile, *M* for metaphor, or *G* if the description is just a general comparison.

Example __M__ Eric watched the blue blossom of gas on the stove.

_____ 1. His thoughts were like hummingbirds buzzing through his head.

_____ 2. Maria's son Carlos is an absolute steamroller of energy.

_____ 3. Grandfather complained that he felt tired as a racehorse.

_____ 4. That bestselling new CD you bought has some terrific songs like "Crazy" on it.

_____ 5. Her mouth was a tiny *O* of surprise when I told her the news.

> **Exercise B** Rewrite the following sentences by including an example of the type of figurative language noted in parentheses.

Example When I told the joke, Julia laughed. (simile)

When I told the joke, Julia laughed as loud as a circus clown.

1. The thunder sounded loud. (metaphor)

_____

2. At the sound of the bell, the whole class jumped. (simile)

_____

3. The road curved sharply. (metaphor)

_____

4. Ray's car moves fast. (simile)

_____

5. Lucia's garden is green. (metaphor)

_____

Copyright © Perfection Learning® All rights reserved.

CHAPTER 5 Developing a Description

Exercise A Read each of the following overall impressions. Then read the list of details that may or may not pertain to the impression. On the blank lines, write the two details from the list that do not quite fit the overall impression.

Example **OVERALL IMPRESSION:** a quiet drive in the country

DETAILS: a meadow with horses beside the road, the stress of the city from the previous day, a radio station playing loud rock music, the slow swaying of the weeping willow trees, the soft white clouds billowing across the sky, a shady creek

the stress of the city from the previous day; a radio station
playing loud rock music

1. **OVERALL IMPRESSION:** an ugly shirt you try to persuade your mother not to buy

   DETAILS: the beautiful buttons on its lapel, a price tag that reads $149.99, a car outside the store that keeps honking its horn, the pink polka dots across the front of the shirt, sleeves made of a scratchy fabric

   _____

   _____

2. **OVERALL IMPRESSION:** a hilarious movie or TV show

   DETAILS: the boring commercials before the show, the terrific comedian who played the lead role, the opening scene that made you laugh uproariously, a joke your sister read in a book that reminded her of the movie, a joke you remember from the movie that you always tell

   _____

   _____

3. **OVERALL IMPRESSION:** a difficult history test that makes you nervous

   DETAILS: a hard essay question about the Bill of Rights, the broccoli-cheese casserole you ate during lunch, the person in front of you who keeps kicking his chair and breaking your concentration, the apple you gave the history teacher on the first day of class, your worry about getting a grade higher than a C, the bumps and ridges in the pencil you keep chewing

   _____

   _____

Exercise B Choose one of your "overall impression" situations. Now write a descriptive paragraph, using vivid and precise details to describe the scene. Be sure to choose a suitable organizational pattern for your description, and include at least one example of both simile and metaphor. Use a separate sheet of paper for your work.

Copyright © Perfection Learning® All rights reserved.

CHAPTER 5 Developing a Description

Exercise A For the following sentences, identify what type of order is being used for the description. On the blank lines provided, write *SP* for spatial, *C* for chronological, *SQ* for sequential, *OI* for order of importance, and *D* for developmental.

_____ 1. Most importantly, you should remember to get plenty of rest when preparing for a test. It is also necessary to remain calm and eat a healthy, balanced breakfast in the morning.

_____ 2. Steven slammed the rickety door of the house, then locked it with a quick turn of the shiny key, and finally took two steps forward.

_____ 3. The old clown's face startled me, with its heavily made-up eyes, its broken wire-rimmed glasses, its chipped red plastic nose, and its fake teeth made from piano keys.

_____ 4. To make my famous cactus chili, you must first simmer the peppery ground beef, then sauté the peppers and onions, and then boil the tomatoes, beans, and fragrant chopped cactus.

Exercise B Read the following list of items about playing miniature golf. Then use a separate sheet of paper to write a paragraph that organizes each detail into a logical and meaningful description. Add at least five details of your own to the details you have been given.

- you do poorly on hole #4, the "sneaky snake"
- father choosing putter—one with green handle
- you decide to pass family in front of you
- the first course is a tiny windmill
- you get hole in one on the 16th green
- your father scores a total of 44
- on hole #16, it begins to rain
- father parking the car in the crowded parking lot
- you choose putter—one with the red handle
- you score a total of 51
- you pay the cashier and go back to the car
- you keep playing, even in the rain
- your favorite hole is #7—ball goes into leprechaun's mouth
- you choose color of ball—bright purple
- your father chooses color of ball—bright orange
- another family in front of you, moving very slowly

  Copyright © Perfection Learning® All rights reserved.

CHAPTER 5   Descriptive Paragraphs: Topic Sentences, Sensory Words

Exercise A For each subject, write a topic sentence. Tell whether your topic sentence gives a negative or a positive impression of the subject.

Example   a stranger on the street

The shabby man shuffled along the street in dirty sneakers and an ankle-length, torn raincoat. (negative)

1. a neighborhood store

   _____

   _____

2. a city bus

   _____

   _____

3. a fountain in the park

   _____

   _____

4. a path through the forest

   _____

   _____

5. a neighbor

   _____

   _____

Exercise B Revise the following paragraph by adding words and phrases that appeal to the senses. Use a separate sheet of paper for your work.

    The abandoned lot in the middle of our block looks like a junkyard. Big piles of bricks fill the back of the lot. On top of the bricks is a heap of boards and chunks of plaster. Damp newspapers cling to the broken bottles, and dented cans are on the ground. Someone left a partially burned mattress right in the front. Someone else left the remains of a sandwich and dried-up skins of fruit. One running shoe and one pump sit neatly side by side. A fender with the words *Wash me* written in the grime adds a final touch to the litter scene.

• • • **CHAPTER 5** **Descriptive Paragraphs: Spatial Order**

Exercise A On the blank line, identify the type of spatial order by writing *near to far*, *top to bottom*, *side to side*, *inside to outside*, or the reverse of any of these. Underline the transitions that make clear the spatial relationships.

Before entering the Metropolitan Museum, I stopped on the steps to view the scene. It had a carnival quality. Close by, businesspeople carrying briefcases, Africans in long flowing gowns, and young people in shorts and sandals moved up and down the wide stairway like ants. Along the broad sidewalk, small tables and benches were lined up under shade trees. Here, mothers allowed their babies to toddle back and forth, while a group of smartly dressed women removed their shoes and twiddled their tired toes. Across the sidewalk, at the edge of the street, vendors with colorful carts were selling cold drinks and popcorn. Beyond, noisy cabs and trucks zoomed past, while bicyclists wove in and out of the heavy traffic. Could the pictures inside the museum possibly be more colorful or entertaining?

Spatial Order: _____

Exercise B Create a character or choose one from a story you have read. Write the character's name. Then brainstorm a list of specific details to describe your character's appearance. Include some figures of speech.

Character: _____

Details: _____

_____

_____

_____

Exercise C Using your brainstorming notes from Exercise B, write a descriptive paragraph. Be sure to include a topic sentence and a concluding sentence. Then revise and edit your paragraph and prepare a neat final copy. Use a separate sheet of paper for your work.

 Copyright © Perfection Learning® All rights reserved.

CHAPTER 5 Writing Descriptive Paragraphs

Exercise A Suppose that you work for a real estate broker who wants to sell an old house to one of two prospective customers. The first is the owner of a film studio that specializes in horror films. The second is a family interested in restoring historic old homes. On a separate sheet of paper, write two descriptive paragraphs about the house, following the directions below.

1. Write two topic sentences. In each, introduce your subjects and set an overall impression.

2. For each paragraph, list specific details and sensory words. List five details and accompanying sensory words that describe the house. Include metaphors and similes.

3. For each paragraph, select a spatial order: *near to far, top to bottom, side to side,* or *inside to outside.* Write three transitions associated with each order.

4. Write a concluding sentence for each paragraph. Summarize the appropriate impression of the house in the concluding sentence.

5. Write two descriptive paragraphs describing the old house. Address one paragraph to the film studio owner; address the other to the family interested in restoration. Use your topic sentences, details and sensory words, order and transitions, and concluding sentences.

6. Revise and edit your paragraphs.

Exercise B Write ten more ideas for descriptive paragraphs.

1. _____   6. _____

2. _____   7. _____

3. _____   8. _____

4. _____   9. _____

5. _____   10. _____

Copyright © Perfection Learning® All rights reserved.

CHAPTER 6 **Elements of a Short Story**

> **Exercise A** Complete this plan for a narrative by writing a possible resolution or outcome.

NARRATOR/POINT OF VIEW: Third-person omniscient

SETTING: A lake in the mountains on a windy day

CHARACTERS AND BRIEF DESCRIPTIONS: Marty and Dolores—Marty is in a sailboat for the first time. Dolores has had a few lessons in sailing. They are in bathing suits and life jackets.

EVENT TRIGGERING ACTION: They are in a small sailboat, 11 feet long. They have sailed down the lake with the wind and are now trying to sail back with the wind pushing them in the opposite direction from their dock.

CONFLICT: Marty wants to let friends in a powerboat tow them to shore. Dolores wants to try to sail back to the dock.

STRUGGLE TO RESOLVE CONFLICT: _____

_____

_____

_____

_____

_____

OUTCOME: _____

_____

_____

_____

> **Exercise B** On a separate sheet of paper, create a plan for a story of your own.

          Copyright © Perfection Learning® All rights reserved.

CHAPTER 6 Writing a Short Story: Sketching Characters/Creating a Setting

Exercise A Write a description of a character for your story. First, complete the following sentences. Then, on a separate sheet of paper, write a paragraph describing your character.

1. The character's name is _____

2. His/Her age is _____

3. His/Her eyes are _____

4. His/Her hair is _____

5. His/Her voice is _____

6. His/Her general size is _____

7. His/Her physical condition is _____

8. His/Her typical mannerisms are _____

9. His/Her background is _____

10. His/Her personality traits are _____

Exercise B Visualize a setting for a short story that reflects both the central conflict and the feelings of the main character. Plan the setting for your story. Include answers to the following questions.

1. Is the setting urban, or is it rural? _____

2. What season of the year is it? _____

3. What time of day is it? _____

4. What is the weather like? _____

5. Where does the action occur, indoors or outdoors? _____

6. If indoors, in what kind of room or building? _____

7. If outdoors, what is the terrain? _____

8. What significant objects are visible? _____

9. What mood are you trying to create? _____

10. What special conditions foretell coming events? _____

_____

CHAPTER 6 Writing a Short Story: The Narrator

Exercise A In the following paragraph, the point of view shifts from third person to first person. Correct this error by using a third-person objective point of view throughout. Mark your corrections on this page.

One day Tom offered to help his uncle build a new railing for the steps leading to the back porch. He kept asking his uncle questions. First, he wanted to know where all the different tools were. As soon as his uncle handed him a hammer, Tom dropped it in the bushes. Then Tom asked where the nails were kept. His uncle told him, but Tom still had trouble finding them. By the time his uncle really had the job well under way, it was getting dark. His uncle and he went closer and closer toward the steps but could barely see what we were doing. The light bulb on the back-porch fixture had such low wattage that it scarcely helped. Then I made a suggestion so good that my uncle looked impressed. I told him to start the engine of his car and finish the job with the help of the headlights.

Exercise B In the following narrative, the narrator tells the story from a third-person objective point of view. On a separate sheet of paper, rewrite the story from a first-person point of view.

Last Monday the Folsoms almost lost a member of the family. Lois got home from school and felt like getting a little fresh air and exercise before doing her chores. Whiffle, their lazy old cat, woke up, yawned, jumped down from his chair, and stretched his front paws out in front of him. Then he looked up at her and said, "Meowowow." That meant, "Let's go for a walk." Off the two of them went, to a park a couple of blocks away.

Lois was watching the fountain, and Whiffle was nosing around in a clump of bushes, when two big dogs came trotting down the path. Suddenly the dogs caught his scent and rushed by Lois into the bushes. At the last second, Whiffle found a tree, and up he went like a jet-propelled squirrel. He came to a stop high above those gleaming white teeth. The dogs finally ran off. Lois called to Whiffle, but he wouldn't come down. Finally, Lois went home without him.

Next morning he showed up for breakfast and greeted her with a matter-of-fact, "Meow."

  Copyright © Perfection Learning® All rights reserved.

CHAPTER 6 Writing a Short Story: Using Dialogue

Exercise A Using dialogue could help bring to life the following exchange between Sonja and her seatmate in a movie theater. Rewrite the exchange in dialogue form, adding any words that might help develop the characters.

Sonja asked a boy in the second seat in a row on the aisle if the seat next to him was taken. He said it wasn't, so she sat down. Just as the robots were filing out of the spaceship on the movie screen, her seatmate said he wanted to go out and buy a bag of popcorn. He pushed past her, stepping on her toes as he went by. A few minutes later he reappeared and asked her if he'd stepped on her toes when he went out. Not very happy, Sonja answered that he had. He told her he was glad, because it meant he was in the right row.

_____

_____

_____

_____

_____

_____

_____

_____

_____

_____

_____

_____

Exercise B Now write a paragraph that follows the scene above. Include at least three examples of dialogue in the new paragraph.

_____

_____

_____

_____

_____

_____

_____

Copyright © Perfection Learning® All rights reserved.

CHAPTER 6 Writing a Play: Creating Characters

Exercise A Think of characters who are unique or interesting enough to write about in a play. These characters may be based on real-life people you know or have heard about, or may be people wholly from your own imagination. Freewrite about these characters to imagine them in different situations. Use a separate sheet of paper for your work.

Exercise B Choose two of the characters you wrote about in Exercise A. On the lines below, write a character sketch for each. Be sure to answer questions such as: What does my character look like? What kind of personality does my character have? What patterns of speech does he or she have?

CHARACTER #1

_____

_____

_____

_____

_____

_____

_____

_____

_____

_____

_____

_____

CHARACTER #2

_____

_____

_____

_____

_____

_____

_____

_____

_____

_____

_____

_____

  Copyright © Perfection Learning® All rights reserved.

••• **CHAPTER 6** **Writing a Play: Creating Dialogue and Stage Directions**

Exercise A Use the characters you wrote about on the previous page, and imagine them in an interesting situation that presents a conflict. Now write dialogue, using at least three separate speeches for each character. Write only the dialogue; do not include descriptions.

_____

_____

_____

_____

_____

_____

Exercise B Add to the dialogue you just wrote by including at least two examples of stage directions for your characters. Try to decide on directions for your characters that could express aspects of their speeches or actions that the dialogue does not already express.

Exercise C Choose one of the following scene ideas and write a brief one-scene play for the rest of the class to present orally. Use separate sheets of paper. Remember to include unique and interesting characters and use natural-sounding, focused dialogue. When you have finished writing your scene, be sure to revise and edit your draft. Then share your final scene with your classmates, and have them present your play to the rest of the class.

a memorable Thanksgiving dinner	why I love chocolate
an allergy	a visit to the dentist
afraid of the dark	a trip to the ocean
my most embarrassing moment	finding something that was lost

Copyright © Perfection Learning® All rights reserved.

CHAPTER 6 Writing a Poem

Exercise A Read the following possible ideas for subjects for poems. Then, for each category, write down specific ideas of your own in the spaces provided.

EVENTS: the circus; learning to dance; doing the dishes; going to the dentist

_____

SCENES: a swimming pool on a hot day; a creepy old house; a busy supermarket

_____

SENSATIONS: eating cotton candy; a puppy licking your face; visiting old friends; the sound and
                 smell of a storm

_____

Exercise B For each sound device, list two examples to use in writing your poem.

---

1. **Onomatopoeia** _____

   _____

2. **Alliteration** _____

   _____

3. **Consonance** _____

   _____

4. **Assonance** _____

   _____

Exercise C Explore figurative language to use in writing your poem. Write an example of each of the following.

---

1. **Imagery** (use of concrete details to create a picture and appeal to the senses)

   _____

2. **Simile** (comparison between unlike things, using *like* or *as*)

   _____

3. **Metaphor** (implied comparison between unlike things)

   _____

4. **Hyperbole** (use of exaggeration or overstatement)

   _____

 Copyright © Perfection Learning® All rights reserved.

CHAPTER 7 — Developing a Working Thesis

Exercise Study the items following each subject. Then write a working thesis for an essay to inform.

natural bait
- small live fish
- worms, grasshoppers, shrimp
- dead fish, fish eggs, bread

artificial bait
- lures made of feathers, hair, or yarn
- wooden or plastic lures made to resemble fish or frogs
- spinners or spoons

WORKING THESIS:

_____

_____

_____

forests
- forest canopy—tops of trees
- understory—trees shorter than those in canopy
- shrub layer—mostly shrubs
- herb layer—ferns, grasses, wildflowers
- forest floor—moss, waste from upper layers

WORKING THESIS:

_____

_____

_____

high school
- freedom in selecting courses
- individual schedule of classes and activities
- use of homeroom system

elementary school
- same classes for everyone
- same schedule for everyone
- spend most of day in one classroom

WORKING THESIS:

_____

_____

_____

Copyright © Perfection Learning® All rights reserved.

CHAPTER 7 Organizing Your Essay

Exercise Read the following informative essay and answer the questions that follow it.

The United States has many monuments that are familiar to all of its citizens. Such landmarks include the Washington Monument, the Statue of Liberty, the Capitol, and the Empire State Building. One unusual monument recognized by most Americans is the colossal memorial carved in the face of Mount Rushmore in South Dakota.

In 1927, the sculptor Gutzon Borglum began the work of creating portraits in stone of four United States presidents—George Washington, Thomas Jefferson, Abraham Lincoln, and Theodore Roosevelt. The work stretched out over a period of fourteen years because of delays caused by weather and lack of funds.

Creating portraits measuring sixty feet from top of head to bottom of chin required engineering techniques as well as traditional techniques of sculpture. The rough shape of each head was formed by blasting away sections of rock as thick as one hundred twenty feet. In addition, the exposed rock surface was then jackhammered, drilled, or chiseled to mold features on each face. Finally, these were smoothed with an air gun and drill bit.

Gutzon Borglum worked hard during his years at Mount Rushmore. However, he did not live to see the completion of his work. After his death in 1941, his son, Lincoln Borglum, carried on the work for a year. After a year, work was not so much completed as simply stopped.

Today the monument is visited by millions of tourists. The presidential portraits have captured a piece of the American spirit.

1. Which sentence states the thesis?

_____

2. What examples of other national monuments are given in the introduction?

_____

3. What are two examples of transitions used by the author in the body of the essay?

_____

4. Give an example of one specific detail provided by the author.

_____

5. Does the conclusion summarize the body of the essay, restate the thesis, draw a conclusion, or add an insight?

_____

   Copyright © Perfection Learning® All rights reserved.

CHAPTER 7 Making an Outline

Exercise Complete the outline about why eating habits differ, using the following unsorted entries.

Use of chopsticks	Cold areas
Use of different seasonings	Days of fasting
Climate	Customs
Near sea	Inland areas
Serving of food	

I. Geographic reasons

   A. Location

      1. _____

      2. _____

   B. _____

      1. Tropical regions

      2. _____

   C. Physical features

II. Religious reasons

   A. Groups that don't eat certain foods

   B. _____

III. _____

   A. Traditional dishes

   B. Use of different cooking methods

   C. _____

IV. _____

   A. Use of knives, forks, and spoons

   B. _____

   C. Use of bread or fingers as utensils

Copyright © Perfection Learning® All rights reserved.

• • • CHAPTER 8   Confusing Fact and Opinion

Exercise A On the blank line, label each statement *F* (fact) or *O* (opinion).

Example   ___O___   Springfield is the best city to live in.

_____ 1. I should have gotten an A on that test.

_____ 2. New Year's Day falls on a Tuesday this year.

_____ 3. A cat makes a better pet than a dog.

_____ 4. John Le Carré writes wonderful spy novels.

_____ 5. I saw the full moon in the east last night.

_____ 6. Several species of ants make slaves of other ants.

_____ 7. The capital of Spain is Madrid.

_____ 8. John Le Carré wrote the novel *The Spy Who Came in from the Cold.*

_____ 9. Spiders in the house are a nuisance.

_____ 10. John James Audubon painted pictures of birds.

_____ 11. A Marion's tortoise may live 152 years or more.

_____ 12. Audubon's bird paintings are wonderful to look at.

_____ 13. Summer is my favorite season.

_____ 14. Drums are too loud and noisy.

_____ 15. Summer is the best season of all.

_____ 16. Drums come in many different shapes and sizes.

_____ 17. Cheese is my favorite food.

_____ 18. My sister was born in 1988.

_____ 19. The restaurant in the next block makes excellent sandwiches.

_____ 20. My sister is a very pretty girl.

Exercise B In the space below, write one fact and one opinion on the same subject.

Subject _____

Fact _____

_____

Opinion _____

_____

Copyright © Perfection Learning® All rights reserved.

CHAPTER 8   Understanding Facts and Opinions: Generalizations

Exercise A Identify each statement by writing *F* (fact) or *O* (opinion) on the blank line.

Example ___F___ The ozone layer helps protect us from getting sunburned.

_____ 1. Suntans look beautiful.

_____ 2. Computers speed up the process of making an airline reservation.

_____ 3. Eating vitamin pills daily makes you healthier.

_____ 4. Seashells are the skeletons of soft-bodied animals.

_____ 5. Chile is east of Washington, D.C.

_____ 6. Walking under a ladder is unlucky.

_____ 7. Everyone should own a computer.

_____ 8. "Calvin and Hobbes" is my favorite cartoon.

_____ 9. "Garfield" is the funniest cartoon.

_____ 10. Every high school student deserves a college education.

Exercise B Rewrite each of the following generalizations to make a revised generalization with which you agree.

Example The ability to use a computer is essential in any job.
> The ability to use a computer is essential in many jobs.

1. All politicians spend taxpayers' dollars recklessly.

_____

2. The best area in which to live is the Southwest.

_____

3. People in the Midwest never see an ocean.

_____

4. American-made cars are better than foreign-made ones.

_____

5. Tennis is a better form of exercise than golf.

_____

Copyright © Perfection Learning® All rights reserved.

CHAPTER 8 Bandwagon Appeals, Testimonials, and Unproved Generalizations

Exercise A Label each statement *B* (bandwagon), *T* (testimonial), or *G* (unproved generalization).

Example __G__ For beautiful, white teeth, the smartest people use Myers Toothpaste.

_____ 1. You can always depend on a Clarkson Watch for accurate time-keeping.

_____ 2. I'm Joe Starbuck, quarterback for the Denver Reds. Use Brown's Musclerub for relief from sore muscles. I do.

_____ 3. Everyone who is anyone is going to Patton Amusement Park for the best rides at the best prices.

_____ 4. Join the health-minded athletes of today at Clark's Gym for the best workout in town.

_____ 5. All the tennis players at Walker Park recommend Hurd tennis rackets.

_____ 6. I'm Max Caldwell, winner of the Sportsway Speed Car Trophy. I always buy Allan Tires for a safe ride.

_____ 7. After a drink of Sparkle Soda, I always feel strong and lively.

_____ 8. The smart set uses Dell's Hairspray. Try it and you, too, will be part of the smart set.

_____ 9. All of your hard cleaning jobs will be made easier if you use Derr Cleaning Powder. Try it today.

_____ 10. Hi! My name is Pedro Castinada, star of stage and screen. I buy my eyeglasses at Vista Vision, the store with fast service and better prices.

Exercise B Write a bandwagon, testimonial, or unproven generalization for an imaginary product or service. Label your statement *B*, *T*, or *G*.

_____

_____

_____

_____

_____

_____

   Copyright © Perfection Learning® All rights reserved.

CHAPTER 8 Persuasive Paragraphs: Facts, Examples, and Opinions

Exercise A For each of the following statements, write *F* if it states a fact or *O* if it states an opinion.

Example __F__ Conservationists are working to save many endangered species.

_____ 1. Conservationists should work harder to save the dolphin.

_____ 2. Many high school students participate in team sports.

_____ 3. Using city buses helps keep private cars off our city streets.

_____ 4. Everyone in the city should use city buses.

_____ 5. Every high school student should join a team.

Exercise B The following topic sentences present different views on the subject of cooking. Under each topic sentence, write three facts, examples, or reasons that could be used to support each opinion.

1. **TOPIC SENTENCE:** Anyone can learn to cook.

   a. _____

   _____

   b. _____

   _____

   c. _____

   _____

2. **TOPIC SENTENCE:** Cooks are born, not made.

   a. _____

   _____

   b. _____

   _____

   c. _____

   _____

Copyright © Perfection Learning® All rights reserved.

CHAPTER 8 Persuasive Paragraphs: Order of Importance, Transitions

Exercise A In the following paragraph, underline the transitions that show the relationship between ideas.

Learning to change a tire can save you time, perhaps embarrassment, and most important, money. You may get a flat when you are in a rush to keep a date. You may or may not be lucky enough to have someone stop and help you. Moreover, that someone may not arrive for a long time. If you can't change a tire, you may have to call a garage miles away, and you may not be able to afford the mechanic's charge. In addition to the charge, you will have to pay for the mechanic's mileage from the garage to the spot where you are. How much better it would be to be able to change the tire yourself.

Exercise B Choose one of the topic sentences below or one of your own. On a separate sheet of paper, brainstorm a list of facts, examples, or reasons to support your opinion. Then organize your details in the order in which you wish to present them.

1. Our school needs a swimming pool.

2. Credit should be given for participation in extracurricular activities.

3. More time should be given for moving between classes.

4. Our school needs a larger parking space.

5. Geography should be a required subject in our high school.

Exercise C Write a draft of your paragraph. Remember to avoid using opinions in your supporting sentences. Use polite and reasonable language.

Exercise D Revise and edit your paragraph carefully. Then prepare a neat final copy.

          Copyright © Perfection Learning® All rights reserved.

CHAPTER 8   Writing Persuasive Paragraphs

Exercise A Assume you want to join the school debating team. On the bulletin board, you see the following notice. Use it as the basis for completing the exercise on this page and the next.

ATTENTION DEBATERS!

TRYOUTS FOR DEBATING TEAM—
Monday, September 24
3:15
Auditorium

To qualify for the tryout, submit a written paragraph on one of the topics below. You may argue in favor of the opinion, or against it. Leave the paragraph in Ms. Cronin's mailbox by Wednesday, September 19. You must submit the paragraph in order to be considered for the debate team.

LIST OF TOPICS—Choose one

• Foreign languages should not be required courses.

• Small towns make better homes than big cities do.

• Student exchange programs improve relations between countries.

1. Select your topic. Decide which topic is most interesting to you. Then decide whether you agree or disagree with the opinion.

2. List facts, examples, and reasons that support your point of view.

   _____

   _____

   _____

   _____

   _____

   _____

3. Distinguish fact from opinion. Decide whether each point you listed is a fact or an opinion. Cross out all opinions.

continued

Copyright © Perfection Learning® All rights reserved.

Chapter 8: Writing Persuasive Paragraphs *continued*

4. Write a topic sentence for the topic you chose on the previous page.

_____

5. On a separate sheet of paper, arrange your arguments in order of importance. Number your list of arguments from least to most important.

6. Avoid loaded words. Remove all emotional, insulting, and biased words from your arguments. Substitute polite, reasonable language.

7. State your arguments in order, adding transitions to make the order clear. Write each set of arguments as sentences, in order of importance, after the topic sentence. Refer to the textbook for some common transitions.

8. Write a concluding sentence summarizing your position.

_____

_____

9. Revise and edit your paragraph. Follow the revising and editing guidelines in your textbook.

Exercise B Write ten ideas for persuasive paragraphs.

1. _____   6. _____

2. _____   7. _____

3. _____   8. _____

4. _____   9. _____

5. _____   10. _____

   Copyright © Perfection Learning® All rights reserved.

CHAPTER 8 Developing an Argument

Exercise After each thesis statement the word *pro* or *con* is in parentheses. Write two facts, examples, or reasons that support the thesis statement (pro) OR two that disprove it (con).

Example THESIS STATEMENT: All national and state parks should charge entrance fees. (pro)

This would help keep them in good condition.

This would reduce the number of visitors.

1. **THESIS STATEMENT:** Motorcyclists should be required to keep their lights on while driving. (pro)

_____

_____

2. **THESIS STATEMENT:** Builders should be required to preserve the environment. (con)

_____

_____

3. **THESIS STATEMENT:** Every United States citizen should be guaranteed full medical insurance. (pro)

_____

_____

4. **THESIS STATEMENT:** Dolphins should be kept in marine parks for entertainment and education. (con)

_____

_____

5. **THESIS STATEMENT:** Owners should not have to keep their dogs leashed or confined all the time. (con)

_____

_____

6. **THESIS STATEMENT:** Every city should have green places. (pro)

_____

_____

Copyright © Perfection Learning® All rights reserved.

CHAPTER 8 · Organizing an Argument

> **Exercise A** Below each thesis statement are three supporting ideas. Number the ideas in order of importance, with *1* being least important and *3* being most important. Be ready to justify your answers.

1. **THESIS STATEMENT:** Everyone should be required to take swimming lessons.

   _____ Playing water polo is fun.

   _____ The life you save might be your own.

   _____ Swimming is excellent exercise for the whole body.

2. **THESIS STATEMENT:** Learning a second language has many advantages.

   _____ At least two languages are spoken in many neighborhoods.

   _____ Many citizens travel to foreign countries for work or pleasure.

   _____ Excellent foreign films are shown in most cities.

3. **THESIS STATEMENT:** Public transportation is a great asset for any community.

   _____ Commuting expense is decreased.

   _____ Gasoline consumption is diminished.

   _____ Traffic congestion is lessened.

4. **THESIS STATEMENT:** Developing good eating habits helps you stay healthy.

   _____ Eating too much fat may give you a weight problem.

   _____ Many serious diseases result from an improper diet.

   _____ Eating the proper foods increases your energy and strength.

5. **THESIS STATEMENT:** Forests are a valuable natural resource.

   _____ Most homes are made of lumber.

   _____ Forests provide homes to many animals.

   _____ Trees help provide the oxygen we breathe.

 Copyright © Perfection Learning® All rights reserved.

CHAPTER 9 Responding from Personal Experience

Exercise Read the following poems and then follow the directions on the next page to begin a critical essay about the poem of your choice. Remember to save your work after each exercise.

The Road Not Taken

Two roads diverged in a yellow wood,
And sorry I could not travel both
And be one traveler, long I stood
And looked down one as far as I could
To where it bent in the undergrowth;

Then took the other; as just as fair,
And having perhaps the better claim,
Because it was grassy and wanted wear;
Though as for that, the passing there
Had worn them really about the same,

And both that morning equally lay
In leaves no step had trodden black.
Oh, I kept the first for another day!
Yet knowing how way leads on to way,
I doubted if I should ever come back.

I shall be telling this with a sigh
Somewhere ages and ages hence:
Two roads diverged in a wood, and I—
I took the one less traveled by,
And that has made all the difference.

—Robert Frost

Dreams

Hold fast to dreams
For if dreams die
Life is a broken-winged bird
That cannot fly.

Hold fast to dreams
For when dreams go
Life is a barren field
Frozen with snow.

—Langston Hughes

continued

Chapter 9: **Responding from Personal Experience** *continued*

> **Exercise** Write one or two sentences to answer each of the following questions about "The Road Not Taken" or "Dreams."

1. Do you identify with the imagery of the poem? Why or why not?

   _____

   _____

   _____

   _____

2. How does the poem make you feel? Why?

   _____

   _____

   _____

   _____

3. What personal experiences come to mind as you read this poem?

   _____

   _____

   _____

   _____

4. Is there anything about this poem that puzzles you? If so, why?

   _____

   _____

   _____

   _____

   Copyright © Perfection Learning® All rights reserved.

• • • CHAPTER 9 Responding from Literary Knowledge

Exercise A Choose a poem from page 61 that you would like to analyze and write about. Then write one or two sentences to answer each of the questions below as it pertains to your poem. Use a separate sheet of paper if necessary.

1. What is the title of the poem you have chosen?

   _____

2. How would you describe the persona of the poem?

   _____

3. How does the poem's meter add to the feeling the poem conveys?

   _____

   _____

   _____

   _____

4. Are there any sound devices found in the poem? How do they contribute to the overall effect?

   _____

   _____

   _____

   _____

5. What figures of speech are used in the poem? Describe them.

   _____

   _____

   _____

   _____

6. What is the theme, overall feeling, or message of the poem?

   _____

   _____

   _____

   _____

continued

Chapter 9: Responding from Literary Knowledge *continued*

> **Exercise B** Read a story and evaluate it by answering the following questions.

Story title: _____

Author's name:_____

1. What is the central conflict in the story and how is it resolved or concluded?

   _____

   _____

2. What is the climax, or high point?

   _____

3. What is the main character's motivation, or reason, for behaving as he or she does?

   _____

   _____

4. From whose point of view is the story told?

   _____

5. How did you identify with a character, situation, or feeling?

   _____

   _____

6. How does the setting contribute to the meaning of the story?

   _____

   _____

7. What do you think is the theme, the main idea, meaning, or message of the story?

   _____

   _____

8. Did you enjoy the story? Why or why not?

   _____

   _____

continued

  Copyright © Perfection Learning® All rights reserved.

Chapter 9: Responding from Literary Knowledge *continued*

Exercise C Choose a poem or short story to read. After reading, write a thesis statement or interpretation for a literary analysis of the poem or short story you have chosen. Complete the chart below with specific examples of description, action, and thoughts. Also include a brief note explaining how each detail helps support the thesis. Remember to limit your details to those that support the point you are making. Use a separate sheet of paper if you need additional space.

DESCRIPTION

Detail: _____

_____

_____

Detail: _____

_____

_____

Detail: _____

_____

_____

ACTION

Detail: _____

_____

_____

Detail: _____

_____

_____

THOUGHTS

Detail: _____

_____

_____

Detail: _____

_____

_____

CHAPTER 10 Limiting a Research Subject

Exercise For each general subject, write three limited subjects.

Example hobbies: _collecting shells_   _building mobiles_   _knitting_

1. deserts:

   _____

   _____

   _____

2. plants:

   _____

   _____

   _____

3. weather:

   _____

   _____

   _____

4. horseback riding:

   _____

   _____

   _____

5. cooking:

   _____

   _____

   _____

6. animal life:

   _____

   _____

   _____

7. medical research:

   _____

   _____

   _____

8. computers:

   _____

   _____

   _____

9. winter sports:

   _____

   _____

   _____

10. public utilities:

   _____

   _____

   _____

Copyright © Perfection Learning® All rights reserved.

CHAPTER 10 Using the Dewey Decimal System

Exercise On the blank line, write the range where you would look to find each item. Use the chart of the Dewey Decimal system below.

Dewey Decimal System		
000–099 General References	**500–599**	Natural Sciences (math, biology, chemistry)
100–199 Philosophy and Psychology	**600–699**	Technology (medicine, inventions)
200–299 Religion	**700–799**	Arts (painting, music, theater)
300–399 Social Sciences (law, education, economics)	**800–899**	Literature
400–499 Languages	**900–999**	Geography and History (including biography and travel)

1. a book on airplane design _____

2. *Handmade Jewelry* _____

3. travel in Greece _____

4. *The Story of Buddhism* _____

5. *Modern Computer Design* _____

6. a dictionary _____

7. *Rocketry and Space Travel* _____

8. the development of law schools _____

9. *The Life of the Pond* _____

10. the life of Geronimo _____

11. short stories by Katherine Mansfield _____

12. the philosophy of yoga _____

13. the history of colonial Louisiana _____

14. *The Development of Vaccines* _____

continued

Copyright © Perfection Learning® All rights reserved.

Chapter 10: Using the Dewey Decimal System *continued*

15. poems by Robert Frost _____

16. a novel by John Steinbeck _____

17. how the flute developed _____

18. the life of Golda Meir _____

19. *Our Disappearing Species* _____

20. *Learning to Speak Italian* _____

21. *Understanding Shakespeare* _____

22. a novel by Jane Austen _____

23. Helen Keller's autobiography _____

24. *New Spanish Dictionary* _____

25. *Vietnamese Grammar* _____

26. *The World's Deserts* _____

27. *One-Room Schools of the 1800s* _____

28. *The Philosophy of Thoreau* _____

29. poems of E. B. Browning _____

30. the building of bridges _____

 Copyright © Perfection Learning® All rights reserved.

CHAPTER 10 Using Reference Materials

Exercise A From the list below, choose the best source for finding the answer to each of the following questions. Use the general encyclopedia as an answer only when no other source seems appropriate.

general encyclopedia	book of quotations
specialized encyclopedia	index to poetry
specialized dictionary	atlas
biographical reference	almanac

Example Where is Tanzania? _____ atlas _____

1. Who said, "They laugh that win"? _____

2. Who are some nineteenth century sculptors? _____

3. What is the birthdate of Michelle Obama? _____

4. Who is a recent member of the Baseball Hall of Fame? _____

5. What is Jonas Salk famous for? _____

6. What are the ten highest mountains in the world? _____

7. What are synonyms for *speak*? _____

8. What are the dates of some major earthquakes? _____

9. Who is the author of the statement, "Let us have peace"? _____

10. Who is a recent winner of an Oscar? _____

11. What are the main crops grown in California? _____

12. Which city is nearer the North Pole, New York or London? _____

13. What university was Woodrow Wilson president of? _____

14. Who wrote "Fire and Ice"? _____

15. What are synonyms for *run*? _____

continued

Chapter 10: Using Reference Materials *continued*

> **Exercise B** Write the name of the reference work that could provide the answer to each question below. List each title only once.

> *Dictionary of World Mythology*
> *Readers' Guide to Periodical Literature*
> *Bartlett's Familiar Quotations*
> *National Geographic Atlas of the World*
> *Information Please Almanac*
>
> *The Oxford Companion to American Literature*
> *The New Roget's Thesaurus in Dictionary Form*
> *A Complete Guide to American Colleges*
> *Who's Who in America*
> *Encyclopedia of Textiles*

1. Who wrote the line, "When annual elections end, there slavery begins"?

_____

2. What are the place and date of birth of the American opera singer Leontyne Price?

_____

3. What is the title of a recent magazine article on bicycle safety?

_____

4. Who is Hahgwehdiyu in Iroquois mythology?

_____

5. Is the tuition charge at the University of California lower for residents of that state?

_____

6. What function does a latch needle perform in the production of textiles?

_____

7. What is the world's longest river, and how long is it?

_____

8. Who won the Nobel Prize for physics in 1968, and for what research?

_____

9. What are six synonyms for the noun *motive*?

_____

10. What was the real name of the American story writer O. Henry?

_____

  Copyright © Perfection Learning® All rights reserved.

CHAPTER 10 **Taking Notes and Summarizing**

Exercise A Write the information asked for as it appears in the sample note card.

President Johnson's wife, Lady Bird   **5**

"I felt ten pounds lighter, ten years younger, and full of plans." (Lady Bird Johnson, p. 493)

—helped her husband manage their ranch and broadcasting properties

—happy that President Johnson decided not to seek another term in 1968

—crusaded for beautifying U.S. countryside

—in 1965, inspired a law restricting billboards on interstate highways

---

1. Aspect of subject _____

2. Source number _____

3. Author of direct quotation _____

4. Number of main points summarized _____

5. Page number in source book _____

Exercise B Write a note card for the following encyclopedia entry on another sheet of paper.

John Wilkes Booth (1838–1865) assassinated President Abraham Lincoln at Ford's Theatre in Washington, D.C., on April 14, 1865. Booth, an actor of promise, had been sympathetic with the Southern cause in the Civil War. He learned that Lincoln was to attend a performance of *Our American Cousin*. He entered Lincoln's private box a few minutes after 10 P.M., and shot him through the head. Booth then leaped to the stage below, shouting, "Sic semper tyrannis! (Thus always to tyrants!)" Booth broke his leg in the leap, but escaped through a back door, mounted a horse, and fled through Maryland. He was hunted down and shot in a barn near Port Royal, VA, for this crime. It is commonly believed that he was emotionally unbalanced. He was born in Bel Air, MD.

—*William Van Lennep*,
The World Book Encyclopedia

---

continued

Copyright © Perfection Learning® All rights reserved.   Grade 9 • Chapter 10: Research: Planning and Gathering Information **71**

Chapter 10: Taking Notes and Summarizing *continued*

> **Exercise C** Write brief summaries of the following statements.

1. Deserts may be hot, dry, sandy areas or cold, rocky, snowy, or icy areas where few living things exist.

   _____

   _____

   _____

2. Sir Arthur Conan Doyle, the creator of Sherlock Holmes, was a doctor who became a writer because he couldn't make a living in medicine.

   _____

   _____

   _____

3. Whooping cranes spend the summer in the Northwest Territories of Canada and the winter along the Gulf Coast of Texas.

   _____

   _____

   _____

4. Egypt's Aswan High Dam saves water for farmers to irrigate with year-round, and it provides power to create electricity.

   _____

   _____

   _____

5. Fossil remains of dinosaur bones and teeth, which scientists say are 150 million years old, have been dug up in many parts of the world.

   _____

   _____

   _____

Copyright © Perfection Learning® All rights reserved.

CHAPTER 11 Organizing Your Notes

Exercise Assume that you have been asked to write a research paper that will cast a fresh look at something that is part of everyday life, such as paper bags. Study the following sources and note cards. Then follow the directions in each exercise to write an outline for a research paper.

1. *Encyclopedia of Inventions*. Philadelphia: Tri-Crown, 1983.

2. Levy, Joel. *Really Useful: The Origins of Everyday Things*. Buffalo, NY: Firefly Books, 2002.

3. Wadsworth, Glenn. *The Story of Paper*. Chicago, IL: Bremmer Books, 1980.

4. Ernest Mahoney, "The Elegant Paper Bag," *Today's Consumer*, December 9, 1983, 81–87.

5. Julia Lee, "Kinds of Paper Bags," *Shopper's Digest*, July 18, 1984, 19.

6. Shoppers Choose Paper Bags, *Boston Sun*, March 21, 1985.

Early Development: Machines   **1**

—by 1860s several machines invented to make paper bags

—1869, best features of all combined into one machine by Union Company of Pennsylvania

—became Union Bag & Paper Company

—in first year, 1875, made 606 million bags

—1883, Charles Stilwell invented machine to produce automatic bag

p.546

Before Paper Bags   **4**

—bags unknown little more than 100 years ago

—1850s, storekeepers received commodities in bulk, not packaged

—if customer didn't bring container, clerk made paper container

—soon some containers being made up in advance by clerks

p. 81

Copyright © Perfection Learning® All rights reserved.

Chapter 11: Organizing Your Notes *continued*

Main Types   **5**

—*flat bag—small paper tube sealed at one end*

—*square bag—tucks in sides to afford more space*

—*automatic bag or self-opening square—square, flat bottom so can stand open or be folded flat*

—*different specialty bags: for example, protective linings, mothproof, insulated*

p.19

Common Uses   **6**

—*still one of our most useful items*

—*main use—to transport things like groceries*

—*users like to keep for reuse as bags*

—*for storage*

—*for trash*

Decide how to group the information on the notecards into three, four, or five categories. Write the names of the categories on the lines below.

1. _____

2. _____

3. _____

4. _____

5. _____

Decide what kind of order is best suited to your subject. Then write a Roman numeral next to each category above to show this order.

Copyright © Perfection Learning® All rights reserved.

CHAPTER 11 Outlining

> **Exercise** Complete the outline below. Use the following unsorted entries.

Kinds of fire departments	Fire-alarm box
Ladder trucks	Public education program
Paid departments	Home building inspections
Fire-related emergencies	Fighting a building fire
Alarm headquarters	Volunteer departments

I. The work of a fire department

   A. Fire fighting

      1. _____

      2. Fighting a grassland or forest fire

   B. Emergency rescue operations

      1. Nonfire emergencies

      2. _____

      3. Paramedic units

   C. Fire prevention and safety

      1. Public building inspections

      2. _____

      3. _____

II. Fire department equipment

   A. Communication system

      1. _____

      2. Automatic signals

      3. _____

   B. Fire trucks

      1. Pumpers

      2. _____

      3. Rescue trucks

      4. Special vehicles

III. _____

   A. _____

   B. _____

   C. Special purpose departments

Copyright © Perfection Learning® All rights reserved.